Ketogenic Instant Pot Cookbook

Sophia Rose

Table of Contents

Introduction

Thank you for taking the time to download the *Ketogenic Instant Pot Cookbook*. If you have read my other book on 'Ketogenic Fat Bombs' then you will love this new one.

I am so glad that you have chosen to take a new path using the ketogenic diet plan along with your handy Instant Pot.

This book is designed to cater for people of all ages. You will find it is suited to the family orientated person and also the hard training athlete. This is a great way to live a healthy lifestyle as well as being extremely time efficient.

The plan goes by many different names such as the keto diet, the low-carbohydrate diet & high-fat (LCHF) diet plan or simply just a low- carb diet. Your liver produces ketones which are used as energy to provide adequate levels of protein similar to other low carbohydrate diet techniques. The process known as ketosis is natural and happens every day – no matter the total of carbs consumed.

First, let's better understand how the plan was discovered and its progress.

Brief History

In 1924, Dr. Russell Wilder from the Mayo Clinic designed the keto plan which was used as part of an epilepsy therapy treatment plan since he also suffered from epilepsy. The plan became known for its other effects which helped in weight loss, and many other ailments.

The program for ketosis was set aside in the 1940s because newer methods were invented for the treatment of epilepsy. However, during that time, 20-30% of the cases using the alternate plan had failed. Therefore, the ketogenic plan was reintroduced to the patients.

As of 2018, Wilder is still functioning successfully without the seizure episodes. The ketogenic plan is especially recommended for children that suffer from being overweight in this current day and age though.

The Keto Diet Plans

If you are a beginner, you will soon discover how flexibility or strictness is the name of the dieting game. Its all about keeping a healthy life balance with your food, not just a quick 8-week diet. Depending on your circumstances, you may not want to have the same goals as another individual. These are the four plans, so you are aware of the different possible levels while using the ketogenic diet techniques:

Keto Method 1: The standard ketogenic diet (SKD) consists of high-fat, moderate protein, and is low in carbs. (For normal family orientated people)

Keto Method 2: The targeted keto diet, which is also called TKD, will provide you with a technique to add carbs to the diet plan during the times when you are working out. (for the low-moderate level athlete)

Keto Method 3: The cyclical ketogenic diet or CKD is observed with five-keto days followed by two high-carbohydrate days. (for moderate level athlete)

Keto Method 4: The high-protein keto diet is comparable to the standard keto plan (SKD) in all aspects. However, it does have more protein. (for the more advanced athlete that trains 4-5 times a week)

If you are a beginner, you will be using the first method. At the completion of this book, you will have a good understanding of how to prepare meals for your family using the ketogenic diet plan with the use of your Instant Pot.

Once again, thanks for downloading this book, and I hope you find it to be helpful!

Chapter 1: The Ketogenic Diet Plan

Before starting your new way of life, (not a fad 8-week diet) there are a few pointers which can help you better understand how the keto diet plan can benefit you and or your family.

Terminology Used

As you begin your journey through the keto world, you will come across many terms or abbreviations that may seem foreign. These are a few:

- Extra-virgin olive oil (EVOO)
- Heavy Whipping Cream (*HWC)* is used by many cooks.
- Low-Carb and High-Fat (*LCHF*)
- Sugar-Free (*SF*) Artificial Sweetener (*AS*) provides a zero/reduced carb count
- Bulletproof Coffee (*BPC*) is generally a mixture of coffee, oil, and butter. It is meant to give you a full feeling.

You will be using extra-virgin olive oil (EVOO) for many of the recipes. You can make your own spray for using the olive oil spray by adding the oil to a spray bottle. You can also use canola oil which is also a good choice for baking.

Essential Foods for the Ketogenic Diet Plan

It is very important to increase your salt intake while you are on the ketogenic diet. The ketones act as a diuretic. Therefore, you lose magnesium, salt, calcium, and potassium. When the carbs are restricted, the kidneys excrete sodium. You must replace the sodium, or you may become light headed.

Try having a large glass of spring water with about ½ teaspoon of Celtic sea salt twice a day. It is best when done first thing in the morning and the midafternoon hours. Add that salt to your meals to taste.

The Keto "Good" Foods

Pantry Items

These are some of the favorites to use while on the ketogenic diet:

- Coconut flour
- Quinoa
- Splenda & Stevia
- Sugar-free ketchup
- Sugar-free gelatin
- Unsweetened cocoa powder
- Yellow mustard
- Pickles (limit sweet or bread & butter)
- Natural nut butter – no sugar

Preferred Spices

You will need to become a label reader for spices because many of the pre-packaged products contain sugar. Sea salt is preferred over table salt since it is typically mixed with powdered dextrose. Use these items:

- Black Pepper
- Basil
- Cayenne Pepper
- Cinnamon
- Chili Powder
- Cilantro
- Sea Salt

Nuts and Seeds

- Flours from nuts and seeds are good substitutes for regular flour which include milled flax seed and almond flour.

- Almonds, walnuts, and macadamias can be eaten in small amounts and are good for your carb counts.

Dairy Products

It is important to maintain your health using dairy products. It is best to choose fresh/raw or organic milk products. You can also add additional protein and calcium using non-dairy products such as cashew or almond milk. Keep these in the fridge:

- Heavy whipping cream
- Butter
- Cream cheese
- Cottage cheese
- Mozzarella cheese

- Cheddar cheese
- Sour cream
- Ghee
- Parmesan cheese
- Sharp cheddar cheese

Vegetables

Many of the vegetables have a lot of carbohydrates. You will want to consider these:

- Mustard Greens
- Parsley - chopped
- Spinach - raw
- Asparagus - steamed
- Alfalfa Sprouts
- Broccoli Florets
- Cauliflower - steamed
- Fresh Garlic
- Radishes
- Corn kernels
- Parsnips
- Water Chestnuts
- Squash
- Tomatoes - cherry
- Carrots - steamed
- Onions
- Peppers – red or green

- Celery - raw
- Green Beans - steamed
- Tomatoes
- Turnips
- Zucchini
- Yellow Wax Beans
- Eggplant - broiled
- Cabbage - steamed

Protein Products

The keto plan focuses on quality proteins, not carbohydrates. You will see many items listed as a starting point.

- Shellfish: Choose crabs, clams, lobster, oysters, scallops, squid, or mussels.
- Tuna: Fresh and canned
- Salmon: Fresh wild caught salmon – portion in bags to freeze
- Other Fish: Trout, snapper halibut, cod, flounder, mackerel, or mahi-mahi
- Shrimp
- Whole Eggs: Scrambled, fried, deviled, or boiled
- Fresh nuts: Macadamia, sesame seeds, flax seeds, chia seeds, etc.
- Peanut butter: Try natural peanut butter, but use caution because they do contain high counts of carbohydrates and Omega-6s. Macadamia nut butter is a wise alternative.

- Turkey: Breasts & ground turkey
- Pork Chops
- Chicken: Thighs, breasts, drumsticks, & ground chicken
- Beef: Flank steak, chuck roast, sirloin, lean ground beef
- Venison: This is a good choice since it is lean and vegetarian raised meat.
- Meat: Grass-fed is preferred because it has a better fatty acid count. Choose from lamb, beef, veal, goat, or other wild game.
- Poultry: Duck, quail, chicken, or pheasant
- Bacon and Sausage: Avoid bacon and sausage that have extra fillers or have been cured in sugar.
- Pork: Pork chops, pork loins, and ham are good options. However, you also have to beware of the added sugar

Healthy Fats

To achieve success in the ketogenic diet, you need fats. Fats are an important part of your diet, but it is important to know which ones are beneficial to your health and the ones that can be dangerous. You need to balance your Omega-3's and Omega-6's.

Salmon, shellfish, trout, and tuna are good for the Omega-3 balance. If you dislike fish, you could try fish oil supplements or take krill oil.

Monounsaturated and Saturated Fats include avocado, butter, coconut oil, egg yolks, and macadamia nuts are some of the recommended categories. These products can be incorporated into your meals using dressings, sauces, or a bit of butter on your meat.

Use non-hydrogenated lard, coconut oil, ghee, or beef tallow. Less oxidation occurs in the oil because they have higher smoke points than other oils. These are some of those:

- Avocado
- Butter or Ghee
- Coconut Butter and Oil
- Red Palm Oil
- Non-hydrogenated lard
- Extra-virgin olive oil (EVOO)
- Chicken Fat
- Mayonnaise (watch the carbs)
- Sesame, avocado, and coconut oil
- Flaxseed oil
- Coconut flakes
- Macadamia nuts
- Olives

Foods to Limit – Be Aware

You may use these sometimes, but try to limit the amounts used. Always count the extra carbs in your recipes; usually shown as optional ingredients.

These are a few of the ones to use occasionally if you have a craving:

- Agave Nectar: One teaspoon has 5 grams of carbs versus 4 grams of table sugar.

- Beans and Legumes: This group to avoid includes peas, lentils, kidney beans, and chickpeas. If you use them; be sure to count the carbs, protein, and fat content.

- Cashews and Pistachios: The high carb content should be monitored for these yummy nuts.

- Fruits: Raspberries, blueberries, and cranberries contain a high sugar content. In small portions; you can enjoy some strawberries, apples, or pears.

- Grains and Starches: Avoid too much grain products including wheat-based items such as cereal, rice, or pasta.

- Hydrogenated Fats: Cold-pressed items should be avoided when using vegetable oils such as safflower, olive, soybean, or flax. Coronary heart disease has been linked to these fats which also include margarine.

- Sweet potatoes

- Potatoes and potato products

- Corn and corn products

- Alcohol Products: You need to limit the intake of your alcoholic drinks to one night per week, the following drinks are worse for you:

    1. Beer
    2. Flavored liquor
    3. Cocktails
    4. Dry Wine
    5. Mixers: Soda, Juice, or coke
    6. Scotch

Many of the professionals have discovered these are more acceptable:

- Whiskey, Barley, corn, rye, and wheat are the grains used which have zero carbs or sugar.
- Tequila: The agave plant is the source of tequila.
- Rum: Choose the ones with zero carbs or sugar.
- Vodka: Check the carb content since it is usually produced (grain-based) from rye, potatoes, and wheat.

This does not promote drinking alcohol, but it does produce ketones in the liver. Remember, it still needs to be consumed in small amounts to prevent any health issues.

You should also avoid sugar including these:
- Dextrose
- Corn syrup
- Fructose
- Honey Maltose
- Maple syrup

Natural Supplements for Ketogenic Dieters

Salt: Use salt to taste on your keto diet plan.

Fermented Foods: Use items while on the keto plan such as coconut milk, kefir coconut milk, yogurt, pickles, olives, sauerkraut, and kimchi to help with any digestive issues.

Lemon and Lime: Your blood sugar levels will naturally drop with these citric additions, and signal a boost in your liver function. Use them in green juices, with a salad, or cooked with meats or veggies. The choices are limitless and assist you with the following:

- Reduces toothache
- Boosts your immune system
- Relieves respiratory infections
- Balances pH
- Decreases wrinkles and blemishes
- Reduces fever
- Excellent for weight loss
- Flushes out the unwanted, unhealthy materials
- Blood purifier

Apple Cider Vinegar: Who would believe the benefits you can receive from just one to two tablespoons of vinegar in an eight-ounce glass of water would help the process? You can choose the straight up method and skip the water. These are just a few ways, and this helps your progress:

- Reduces cholesterol
- Excellent for detoxification
- Helps you to drop the pounds
- Improves your digestion tract
- Helps with sore muscles
- Controls sugar intake/aids in diabetes
- Strengthens your immune system
- A good energy booster
- Balances your inner body system and functions

Cinnamon: Use cinnamon as part of your daily plan to improve your insulin receptor activity. Just put one-half of a teaspoon of cinnamon into a shake or any type of keto dessert. As you will see, many of the keto recipes contain the ingredient.

Turmeric: Dating back to Ayurveda and Chinese medicine, this Asian orange herb has been known for its anti-inflammatory compound. Add it to your smoothies, veggies, green drinks, meats, or veggies. These are some of its benefits:

- Prevents Alzheimer's disease
- Weight management
- Relieves arthritis
- Reduces your cholesterol levels
- Helps control diabetes
- Improves your digestion

The creation of a menu can be a little daunting when you first begin your challenge of preparing and sticking to a ketogenic diet plan. This list is here so you can incorporate some variety while still watching the elements that make up the plan—low carbs—high fat—and high protein.

As you become adjusted to counting these elements, you can plan your meals ahead of time and remove the worry.

Chapter 2: Benefits of the Plan & the Instant Pot

The keto plan is one of the healthiest diets on today's market. It is well worth the few extra minutes it takes to select the menu plan. The ketogenic diet is an excellent plan and aids our health in many ways. This segment shows you a few of those benefits as well as a breakdown of how the carbs work with weight loss.

Health Benefits of the Keto Diet Plan

Improved Thinking Skills: Your brain is approximately 60% fat by weight. Therefore, you might become confused as you consume high-fat foods. By increasing your fatty foods intake; you will have better chances to better your mind. It can maintain itself and work at full capacity.

Alzheimer's Disease: The disease's progression can be slowed down and the symptoms reduced with the keto plan.

Cancer: Several types of cancer and slow tumor growths are being treated by
using the keto diet technique.

Epilepsy: Reduced occurrence of seizures have been cited in children who use the ketogenic diet.

Obesity and Overweight People: Many individuals exceed what is considered healthy figures when it comes to weight. It is imperative to use the keto diet plan to get started on the right path for weight loss.

Lower Blood Pressure: It is advisable to speak with your physician about lowering your meds while on the plan. If you begin to feel dizzy; that is one of the first signs the lack of carbs is working. You are headed in the right direction.

Improvement of your Cholesterol Profile: An arterial buildup is generally associated with the triglyceride and cholesterol levels, which have been proven to improve with the keto diet plan.

Prediabetes and Diabetes: Excess fat is removed with the keto plan, which is linked to pre-diabetes, type-2 diabetes, and metabolic syndrome. In one study, insulin sensitivity was improved by 75%. Similar results with type-2 diabetes patients indicated that out of 21 participants, seven were successful in eliminating all of the medications related to diabetes.

Joint Pain and Stiffness: Grain-based foods are eliminated from your diet on the keto plan. It is believed the grains can be one of the biggest causes of pain or chronic illness. After all, it has been said before, "no pain —no grain."

Gum Disease and Tooth Decay: The pH balance in your mouth is influenced by sugar intake. Your gum issues could subside after about three months on a keto diet plan. You will be consuming healthier foods.

Acne: By eating fewer processed foods and less sugar; your insulin levels will be lowered, and the acne should improve.

Lack of Hunger: This enormous benefit occurs because fat is naturally more satisfying than just carbs. You just need to wait a little longer to become satiated after a meal. The high-carbs will cause the full-state to last longer.

Carbs Needed Daily to Lose Weight

To achieve weight loss, you will need to reduce your carbohydrate intake. You will soon realize that the plan will allow you to feel satiated while still losing weight. You merely restrict carb intake including starches such as bread and pasta, as well as sugars. As a result of the keto diet, you will replace them with fat and protein.

Not only will you lose weight, but you will also reduce your blood pressure, triglycerides, and blood sugar.

What works for one person as a 'low-carb' diet, may be too low for another person. It depends on your activity levels, age, body composition, and gender. It may also depend on your metabolic health, food culture, and personal preferences.

If you are more active and have more muscle mass; you can tolerate more carbs versus someone who is sedentary. If people get the metabolic syndrome, he/she may become obese or suffer from type II diabetes whereas the rules change. It is sometimes referred to by the scientists as 'carbohydrate intolerance.'

As mentioned, there's no set rule for carb intake. These are some of the basic guidelines to consider as you blaze the path on the ketogenic diet plan which is effective about 90% of the time:

Moderate Carb Intake: 100-150 Grams Daily
If you are active and lean trying to maintain weight, these are some of the foods to consider:

- Several fruits daily
- All the veggies you can eat
- Healthy starches such as rice, oats, sweet potatoes, and potatoes

50-100 Grams Daily:

- Plenty of veggies
- 2-3 pieces of fruit each day
- Minimal intake of starchy carbs

20-50 Grams Daily:
Losing weight at the rate of 20-50 g daily quickly falls into this category. If you have diabetes, are obese, or metabolically deranged, this is the plan for you. If you are consuming less than the 50 grams daily, your body will achieve a ketosis state which supplies the ketone bodies.

Consider these guidelines:

- Some berries with whipped cream
- Plenty of low-carbohydrate veggies
- Trace carbs from foods including nuts, seeds, and avocados

As you now see, it is important to experiment and categorize where you fall on the scales before you make any changes. Seek your doctor's advice before changing your eating patterns. In some cases, you could reduce the need for some medications.

It is all about good choices for you and your family!

Instant Pot: The Healthy Choice

You will soon discover how family-friendly the Ketogenic diet plan and the Instant Pot is as a team. First, let's discover a bit of history.

As time passes by, technology has introduced many gadgets for kitchens dating all the way back to 1952 when folks were amazed by the West Bend invention of the Electric Bean Pot. In 1936, Irving Naxon, an inventor attempted to patent a cooker inspired by his Grandmother but failed to receive the required patent. In 1940 he received the patent for the Naxon Beanery 'low and slow' cooker.

The new invention of the Instant Pot in 2010 by one of the founders, Robert Wang really opened the door. Since that time, three new models have been improved and released.

The Instant Pot will combine qualities which include a yogurt maker, slow cooker, rice cooker, electric pressure cooker, sauté pan, steamer, and so many more features the competition cannot match.

The recipes will begin to intrigue you the instant you open the first chapter. You will want to stop what you are doing, visit the supermarket, and purchase each of the ingredients you will need to tempt and satisfy your taste buds!

You will be provided with many recipes from breakfast to dinner as well as a few fairly healthy desserts. Most of them will provide you with healthy choices, and some will just be so yummy, you will forget about the calorie counts for just a few minutes.

How to Operate the Instant Pot

The Instant Pot is a multi-function, countertop 11 psi electric cooker that can be used as a rice cooker, slow cooker, steamer, warmer, and pressure cooker. Newer models like *IP-DUO* and *IP-SMART* have browning, sautéing, pasteurization, and yogurt-making functions.

Just in case you decide you want to use the preset buttons versus the manual ones provided, these are what some of the functions provide to make the Instant Pot cooking process even more straightforward:

Timer: The timer function is used when you need to delay the cooking process. You will need to choose the function which you wish to cook with—make adjustments—press the timer button—click the (+) and (-) buttons.

Pressure: This button switches between high and low pressure.

Slow Cooker: You can use this function to set a default to a 4-hour slow-cook time. Adjust the setting for low (190-201°F), regular (194-205°F) or the high setting (199-210°F). Once again, the plus and minus buttons adjust the cooking time.

Yogurt: This is self-explanatory used for individual jars or making the yogurt directly in the pot.

Benefits of Using Your Instant Pot

This is so easy; just set-it-and-walk-away all-in-one cooker. All you need to do is to:

- Prepare the ingredients ahead of time. Place these into the Instant Pot.

- Twist and lock the lid. Seal or unseal steamer valve (depending on function.)
- Set desired function (ex. Pressure cook, Steam, etc.). Set the timer.
- Walk away and return after the prescribed cooking time.
- Release the pressure. Remove the lid.
- Stir in remaining ingredients, if any.
- Ladle dish into serving containers. Garnish as needed. Serve. Eat.

Pressure cooking means that you can cook meals 75% to 100% faster than boiling/braising on the stovetop, and baking/roasting in a conventional oven.

This is especially helpful for vegan meals that entail the use of dried beans, legumes, pulses, etc. Instead of pre-soaking these ingredients for hours prior to use, you can pour these directly into the pot, add water, and pressure cook these for several minutes.

Use Instant Pot to make meals in advance. The machine automatically activates the Keep Warm function after each cooking cycle. This allows you to prepare meals in the morning so that you can come home to a warm dinner. Alternatively, set up the Instant Pot before going to bed - so that breakfast is cooked when you wake up.

These make your recipes much simpler as you will soon see!

Chapter 3: The 14-Day Meal Plan

The ketogenic diet works best when you have a well-planned menu to lose weight and save your valuable time. These are some of the ways you can achieve and maintain ketosis. Each one is listed using ingredient panels using net carbs. This meal plan is for three meals. You can choose to eliminate one of the meals to have better results. It is up to you how you spend the allotted carbs.

Bare in mind with the eating plan you want to be eating every 4 hours, so space out your meals evenly throughout the day to allow your body to break down the meals at its fastest metabolic rate possible.

Day 1

Egg Cups on the Run – 2 grams net carbs

Balsamic Beef Pot Roast - 3 grams net carbs

Chicken Pot Pie Soup - 3.5 grams net carbs

Peanut Butter Chocolate Cheesecake - 5 grams net carbs

Day 2

Broccoli – Ham & Pepper Frittata - 7 grams net carbs

Bruschetta Chicken - 4 grams net carbs
Cauliflower & Cheese – 7 grams net carbs

Carne Adovada - 4.1 grams net carbs

Almond & Coconut Cake – 3 grams net carbs

Day 3

Perfection: The Hard-Boiled Egg – 0.5 grams net carbs

Leg of Lamb - 0.64 grams net carbs

Beef Chili with no Beans - 8 grams net carbs

Chocolate Mini Cakes for 2 – 9 grams net carbs

Day 4

Deviled Egg Salad – 1.31 grams net carbs

Unstuffed Cabbage Roll Soup - 4.3 grams net carbs

Chipotle Pork Roast - 4 grams net carbs

Day 5

Creamy Salsa Chicken - 3.3 grams net carbs

Kimchi Beef Stew -7 grams net carbs

Italian Meatballs - 5 grams net carbs

Carrot & Almond Cake – 4 grams net carbs

Day 6

Sesame Ginger Chicken - 3 grams net carbs
Mashed Potatoes - 1 grams net carbs

Mutton Curry- 6.34 grams net carbs

Country-Style Pork Ribs - 2 grams net carbs

Coconut Pandan Custard – Thai Style – 6 grams net carbs

Day 7

Beef Stroganoff - 7 grams net carbs

White Chicken Chili - 6 grams net carbs

Cauliflower & Buffalo Chicken - 5.4 grams net carbs

Day 8

Mexican Pork Carnitas - 1 gram net carbs

Unstuffed Cabbage Roll Soup – 4.3 grams net carbs

Sesame Ginger Chicken – 3 grams net carbs

Lemon Ricotta Cheesecake – 2 grams net carbs

Day 9

Perfection: The Soft-Boiled Egg - 0.5 grams net carbs

Greek Meatballs in Tomato Sauce - 12 grams net carbs

Smothered Pork Chops – 4.06 grams net carbs

Day 10

Cuban Pork – 2 grams net carbs

Cauliflower Bacon & Cheese Soup - 13.4 grams net carbs

Steak & Cheese Pot Roast - 3.5 grams net carbs

Pork – Noodles & Veggies – 3 grams net carbs

Day 11

Cabbage & Corned Beef - 5.5 grams net carbs

Spaghetti Squash with Meat Sauce – 5 grams net carbs

Whole Chicken & Gravy - 0.7 grams net carbs

Day 12

Italian Sausage Kale Soup - 8 grams net carbs

Barbacoa Beef – 2 grams net carbs

No-Noodle Lasagna – 6 grams net carbs

Peach & Peanut Butter Chocolate Cheesecake – 4 grams net carbs

Day 13

Ham & Bean Soup - 13 grams net carbs

Frozen Chicken Breasts - 0 grams net carbs

Chicken Korma - 6 grams net carbs

Day 14

Shredded Chipotle Beef - 2.2 grams net carbs

Chicken Poblano Soup – 5 grams net carbs

Spicy Pork – Korean Style - 9 grams net carbs

Now you have the plan! See how easy it is to group tasty foods together and still have plenty of ketogenic carbs left over to use as you wish? As you will soon understand, these are guidelines. You can interchange the menu the way you like it as long as you remain within your carbohydrate limits. Each of the recipes offered has the full nutritional panels for your convenience.

I have selected a large variety in the meals to account for those people that dislike the standard meal plan of one meal all week. But if you find that there are far too many dishes to cook in one week, select half of them and cook in bulk. It will save time and money if this is the path you choose.

Please enjoy!

Chapter 4: Beef Inspired Meals

Balsamic Beef Pot Roast

Servings: 10
Total Time: 65 minutes
Nutrition Facts: 393 Calories| 28 grams Fat |30 grams Protein| 3 grams Net Carbs

Ingredients:
1 t. of each:
   -Garlic powder
   -Ground black pepper
1 tbsp. kosher salt
¼ c. balsamic vinegar
½ c. chopped onion
2 c. water
¼ t. xanthan gum
1 boneless (3 lb.) chuck roast

Vegetables of your choice

For the Garnish: Chopped fresh parsley

Directions:
1. Slice the roast in half and season with the garlic powder, pepper, and salt.
1. Prepare the pot using the saute function and brown the meat.
2. Pour in the onion, water, and vinegar. Secure the lid and set for 35 minutes. Natural release the pressure in the Instant Pot.
3. Add the meat to a container and break it apart. Discard fat and use the saute function to simmer the juices in the pot. Add the meat back after whisking in the xanthan gum. Gently stir, and turn off the heat.
4. Garnish as desired and enjoy with your favorite sides.

Barbacoa Beef

Servings: 9
Total Time: 1 hr. 20 min.
Nutrition Facts: 153 Calories| 24 grams Protein| 4.5 grams Fat|
2 grams Net Carbs

Ingredients:
½ med. onion
5 garlic cloves
2-4 chipotles in adobo sauce – to taste
1 lime – juiced
1 tbsp. ground of each:
   -Cumin
   -Oregano
1 c. water
½ t. ground cloves
3 bay leaves
2 ½ t. kosher salt
Black pepper – to taste
3 lb. eye of round/bottom round – fat trimmed away
1 t. oil

Directions:
1. In a blender, puree the onion, garlic cloves, lime juice, water, cloves, chipotles, cumin, and oregano until smooth.
2. Remove all of the fat and chop into 3-inch bits. Season with 2 teaspoons of salt, and a pinch of pepper.
3. Prepare the Instant Pot on the saute setting and add the oil. Brown the meat in batches (5 min.). Add the sauce from the blender along with the bay leaves into the Instant Pot.

4. Secure the lid and set the timer for 65 minutes using the high-pressure setting. Natural or quick release the pressure, and shred the beef with two forks. Reserve the juices, and throw the bay leaves in the trash.

5. Return the meat to the pot with the cumin, salt to taste, and 1 ½ cups of the reserved juices. Serve when hot.

Beef Chili without Beans

Servings: 8
Total Time: 30 min.
Nutrition Facts: Calories 326| 23 grams Protein| 17 grams Fat|
8 grams Net Carbs

Ingredients:
2 lbs. beef
1 can (6 oz.) tomato paste
2 cans tomato sauce (15 oz. each)
2 tbsp. cumin powder
5 tbsp. chili powder
½ c. dried onion flakes/ 1 med. onion chopped
1 t. Tabasco sauce
1 t. garlic powder/ 2 minced cloves
2 t. fine ground sea salt
1 t. powdered/ dried oregano
For Thinning: 1 c. chicken or beef broth

Directions
1. Finely chop the onion. Use the saute function in the Instant Pot to brown the hamburger. Blend in the Tabasco, garlic or onion flakes, cumin, salt, chili powder, and oregano. Mix thoroughly.
2. Empty one cup of the broth in with the burger, but do not stir.
3. Pour in the tomato sauce and paste - but do not stir.
4. Close the top, and use the manual high-pressure setting for 10 minutes. When done, natural release the pressure for 10 minutes, then quick release.
5. Stir and serve.

Beef Stroganoff

Servings: 4
Total Time: 38 min.
Nutrition Facts: 321 Calories| 16 grams Fat| 33 grams Protein|
7 grams Net Carbs

Ingredients:
1 tbsp. oil
1 tbsp. garlic
½ c. diced onions
1 lb. beef/pork stew meat
1 ½ c. chopped mushrooms
1 t. salt
1 tbsp. Worcestershire sauce
½ t. pepper to taste
¾ c. water

Finishing Ingredients:
¼ t. arrowroot starch/cornstarch/xanthan gum
1/3 c. sour cream

Directions:

1. Prepare the Instant Pot using the saute function. Heat the oil and toss in the garlic and onions. Stir a minute and all everything except the sour cream.
2. Secure the lid and set on high pressure for 20 minutes. Natural release.
3. Change to the saute function and stir in the sour cream. Sprinkle in the xanthan gum slowly, stirring as it thickens.
4. Serve and enjoy with some low-carb noodles or cauliflower rice, but add the carbs.

Greek Meatballs with Tomato Sauce

Servings: 6
Total Time: 40 min.
Nutrition Facts: 261 Calories| 16 grams Fat| 15 grams Protein|12 grams Net Carbs

Ingredients for the Meatballs:
1 slightly beaten egg
¼ c. chopped parsley
½ c. finely chopped onion
1/3 c. Arborio rice
Pepper and salt to taste
1 lb. ground beef

Ingredients for the Sauce:
1 c. water
14 oz. diced tomatoes
½ t. of each:
  -Smoked paprika
  -Cinnamon
1 t. dried oregano
¼ t. ground cloves
Pepper & Salt to taste

Directions:
1. Mix all of the fixings for the meatballs, shaping into eight to ten balls. Arrange in a single layer in the pot.
2. Mix the sauce components in a dish and pour over the prepared meatballs.
3. Program the Instant Pot for 15 minutes under high-pressure. When the timer goes off, release the pressure using the natural release option.
4. Remove the meatballs and blend the sauce until smooth with an immersion blender. Pour over the meatballs, garnish, and serve.

Italian Meatballs

Servings: 5
Total Time: 35 min.
Nutrition Facts: 455 Calories| 34 grams Protein| 33 grams Fat|
5 grams Net Carbs

Ingredients for the Meatballs:
1 ½ lb. ground beef – lean
2 tbsp. freshly chopped parsley
2 eggs
½ c. almond flour
¾ c. grated parmesan cheese
¼ t. of each:
  -Garlic Powder
  -Ground black pepper
1 t. of each:
  -Kosher salt
  -Dried onion flakes
1/3 c. warm water
¼ t. dried oregano

Cooking Ingredients:
1 t. olive oil
3 c. 'keto' marinara sauce/sugar-free sauce

Directions:
1. Mix all of the meatball fixings and shape into 15 (2-inch) balls.
2. Add the oil to the Instant Pot and program the saute function. Brown the meatballs by leaving a ½-inch space between each one in the pot. You can also brown them in a skillet first.

3. Pour in the marinara sauce and secure the lid on low-pressure for 10 minutes.

4. Natural release the remainder of the pressure and serve the tasty treat.

Kimchi Beef Stew

Servings: 6
Total Time: 44 min.
Nutrition Facts: 199 Calories|22 grams Protein|8 grams Fat|7 grams Net Carbs

Ingredients:
1 lb. beef cubes – 2-inch bits
2 c. Kimchi
1 c. of each:
   -Dried Shiitake/another mushroom
   -Chopped onion
1 tbsp. of each:
   -Gochujang brown rice pepper paste
   -Gochugaru Korean chili powder/Cayenne pepper
   -Minced garlic
   -Sesame oil
   -Minced ginger
   -Soy sauce/coconut aminos
¼ t. Splenda/favorite sweetener
2 c. water

To Taste: Salt

Ingredients for Finishing:
½ c. of each:
   -Diced green onion
   -Optional: Diced firm tofu

Directions:
1. Empty all of the fixings into your Instant Pot. Prepare on high for 15 minutes and natural release the pressure for 5 minutes. Quick release the remainder of pressure.

2. Toss in the onions and tofu. Adjust the salt and add a bit more gochugaru if desired.

3. Note: The spices should be available at any Superstore such as Walmart.

Shredded Chipotle Beef

Servings: 16/4-5 Cups
Total Time: 95 minutes
Nutrition Facts: 334 Calories |22.6 grams Protein |25.6 grams
Fat| 2.2 grams Net Carbs

Ingredients:
3 lb. beef chuck roast
1 t. black pepper
2 t. salt
1 tbsp. adobo sauce
2 tbsp. olive oil
1 chipotle in adobo – seeds removed or not – chopped
2 t. dried of each:
   -Oregano
   -Cumin
½ t. chili powder
1 c. fresh cilantro – roughly chopped
1 seeded green bell pepper – large chunks
1 peeled – quartered onion
1 c. water.

Directions:

1. Sprinkle the roast with the pepper and salt. Choose the Instant Pot saute function and pour in the oil. Arrange the roast in the pot and saute 3-4 minutes on each side.
2. Spread with the adobo sauce a chipotle pepper. Sprinkle with the chili powder, oregano, and cumin. Toss the cilantro on top. Add the peppers and onions. Pour the water into the pot and secure the lid.
3. Prepare 60 minutes using the high-pressure setting. Natural release and remove the meat. Shred with two forks and discard the veggies.
4. Add the beef back into the juices. Keep warm until ready to serve. Yummy!

Spaghetti Squash with Meat Sauce

Servings: 8
Total Time: 35 min.
Nutrition Facts: 174 Calories | 19.8 grams Protein |6.8 grams Fat | 5 grams Net Carbs

Ingredients:
1 lb. ground beef
1 med. spaghetti squash
1 jar (32 oz.) marinara sauce
Optional: Parmesan cheese

Directions:

1. Prepare the spaghetti squash. (see the recipe under 'Sides')
2. Brown the beef in a skillet and remove from the heat. Add the sauce and heat until warmed. Pull the spaghetti strands from the squash and serve with a topping of the meat sauce and cheese if desired.
3. Note: The counts include the sauce and squash.

Steak & Cheese Pot Roast

Servings: 8
Total Time: 55 min.
Nutrition Facts: 425 Calories | 25.7 grams Fat| 3.5 grams Net Carbs | 46.1 grams Protein

Ingredients:
1 tbsp. oil
2 large onions
8 oz. sliced mushrooms
1-2 tbsp. Montreal steak seasoning/another favorite Keto choice
1 tbsp. butter
½ c. beef stock
3 lb. chuck roast
Optional: Keto cheese of choice – add the carbs

Directions:
1. Program the Instant Pot to saute and pour in the oil. Rub the roast with the seasoning. Saute 1-2 minutes per side. Remove and add the butter and thinly sliced onions. Toss in the mushrooms, peppers, stock, and roast.
2. Choose the manual high-pressure setting for 35 minutes and natural release. Shred the meat, sprinkle with cheese. Use as desired.

Unstuffed Cabbage Roll Soup

Servings: 9
Total Time: 40 min.
Nutrition Facts: 217 Calories| 14.8 grams Fat| 15.6 grams Protein| 4.3 grams Net Carbs

Ingredients:
2 minced garlic cloves
½ small diced onion
1 ½ lb. ground beef – 80/20
¼ c. Bragg's Aminos
1 can of each tomato type:
  -14 oz. diced
  -8 oz. sauce
3 c. beef broth
3 t. Worcestershire sauce
1 med. chopped cabbage
½ t. of each:
  -Pepper
  -Parsley
  -Salt

Directions:
1. Use the saute function on the Instant pot to brown the beef, garlic, and onions. Drain and add back to the pot with the rest of the fixings.
2. Program the unit on the soup function. Natural release the soup for about ten minutes, and quick release the rest of the steam. Stir and serve.

Chapter 5: Chicken Inspired Meals

Bruschetta Chicken

Servings: 4
Total Time: 60 min.
Nutrition Facts: 480 Calories| 26 grams Fat |52 grams Protein|4 grams Net Carbs

Ingredients:
2 tbsp. balsamic vinegar
½ t. sea salt
2 t. minced garlic cloves
1 t. black pepper
1/3 c. olive oil
½ c. sun-dried tomatoes in olive oil
2 lb. chicken breasts – quartered – boneless
2 tbsp. chopped fresh basil

Directions:

1. Whisk the vinegar, oil, garlic, pepper, and salt together. Fold in the tomatoes and basil. Put the breasts in a freezer bag with the mixture for 30 minutes.
2. After that time, add all of the fixings into the Instant Pot and secure the lid. Select the poultry setting (9 min.). Natural release the pressure for five minutes, quick release, and serve.

Cauliflower & Buffalo Chicken

Servings: 6
Total Time: 15 minutes
Nutrition Facts: 344 Calories | 23.8 grams Protein |24.8 grams
Fat | 5.4 grams Net Carbs

Ingredients
2 c. cubed cooked chicken
1 head chopped cauliflower
½ c. buffalo sauce
½ c. ranch dressing
½ block – cubed cream cheese
2 c. shredded cheddar cheese
Pepper & Salt to taste

Directions:
1. Warm up the Instant Pot with the saute function and add the seasonings, cauliflower, chicken, dressing, and buffalo sauce. Stir well.
2. Set the timer for five minutes with a natural release of the pressure.
3. Serve with some chopped green onion and a drizzle of sauce.

Chicken Korma

Servings: 6
Total Time: 32 min.
Nutrition Facts: 256 Calories| 19.0 grams Fat| 14 grams Protein| 6 grams Net Carbs

Ingredients:
1 lb. chicken thighs
½ c. diced tomatoes
1 chopped onion
½ jalapeño/green serrano
5 garlic cloves
1 t. of each:
  -Garam masala
  -Salt
  -Turmeric
  -Minced ginger
½ t. of each:
  -Ground coriander
  -Cayenne pepper
  -Ground cumin
½ c. water

Ingredients for the Finish:
½ c. unsweetened coconut milk
1 t. garam masala
¼ c. chopped cilantro

Directions:
1. Combine all of the veggies and spices. Add to the Instant Pot.
2. Add the chicken and set the timer for 10 minutes (high pressure). Natural release.
3. Remove the chicken and dice. Pour in the garam masala and coconut milk along with the chicken in the pot.
4. Garnish and serve.

Chicken Poblano Soup

Servings: 8
Total Time: 50 min.
Nutrition: 189 Calories|22 grams Protein| 6 grams Fat|5 grams Net Carbs

Ingredients:
1 ½ lb. chicken breasts
2 c. diced cauliflower
5 garlic cloves
3 poblano chopped peppers
1 c. diced onion
1 t. ground of each:
  -Cumin
  -Coriander
¼ c. chopped cilantro
1-2 t. salt – to taste
2 c. water
To Finish: 2 oz. cream cheese

Directions:
1. Chop the chicken into large chunks and chop or dice the veggies. Add all of the fixings into the Instant Pot (omit the cream cheese).
2. Set the timer for 15 minutes (high pressure) and natural release (ten min.).
3. Use tongs to remove the chicken and roughly puree the veggies and soup.
4. Program the saute function and add the cream cheese. Shred the chicken and combine with the soup.
5. Serve when hot.

Chicken Pot Pie Soup

Servings: 6
Total Time: 1 hr.
Nutrition: 432 Calories| 20.5 grams Protein| 35.1 grams Fat|
3.5 grams Net Carbs

Ingredients:
2 tbsp. butter
1 lb. – 1 ½ lb. (thawed) skinless – boneless chicken breasts
¼ of a small diced onion
½ c. mixed veggies
3 c. chicken broth
¼ t. of each

  -Black pepper
  -Pink salt
2 minced cloves of garlic
1 ¾ c. heavy whipping cream
1 oz. cream cheese
¼ t. rosemary
1 t. poultry seasoning
Pinch of thyme
½ t. xanthan gum

Directions:
1. Melt the butter in the Instant Pot using the saute function. Toss in the mixed veggies, and onion. Cook a few minutes until translucent. Add them to a bowl and set to the side.
2. Pour in ½ c. of the broth to deglaze the cooker. Toss in the chicken along with the spices.
3. Close the top and select the poultry setting (15 minutes).

Natural release for six minutes and do a quick release of the rest of the pressure.

4. Shred the chicken and add the rest of the broth, chicken, cream cheese, veggies, and whipped cream into the pot.

5. Switch to the warm cycle and add the xanthan gum. Stir and saute about 10 minutes. Serve when ready.

Creamy Salsa Chicken

Servings: 6
Total Time: 30 min.
Nutrition Facts: 529 Calories| 70.7 grams Protein| 23.9 grams Fat| 3.3 grams Net Carbs

Ingredients:
½ c. chicken broth
2 ½ - 3 lb. chicken breasts
4 oz. cream cheese
1 c. salsa
½ c. cottage cheese
1-2 t. fajita/taco seasoning
Optional Garnishes:
   -Sour cream
   -Shredded cheese
   -Chopped tomatoes
   -Avocado
   -Cilantro

Directions:
1. Arrange the chicken in the Instant Pot with the broth. Prepare on the poultry setting (10 min.). Quick release the top, making sure the chicken is a minimum of 160°F. If done, place in a large container and reserve ½ cup of the juices.
2. Add the rest of the fixings and the ½ cup of broth to the pot.
3. Choose the saute function and whisk the cottage cheese and cream cheese well – until melted.
4. Shred the chicken and add it to the sauce. Serve and garnish to your liking.

Frozen Chicken Breasts

Servings: 4
Total Time: 37 min.
Nutrition Facts: 128 Calories| 23 grams Protein| 2 grams Fat|
0 grams Net Carbs

Ingredients:
1 ¼ c. water
4 chicken breasts – skinless
Spices of your choice
My choice spices for this are parsley and lemon pepper

Directions:
1. Pour the water into the Instant Pot, and add the frozen chicken along with spices
2. Secure the top and set for 10 minutes. Natural release for ten more minutes, and quick release.
3. Open the lid and enjoy!

Sesame Ginger Chicken

Servings: 6
Total Time: 30 min.
Nutrition Facts: 286 Calories|19 grams Protein| 21 grams Fat|
3 grams Net Carbs

Ingredients:
1 ½ lb. chicken thighs – no skin or bones
2 tbsp. liquid aminos
1 tbsp. of each:
    -Agave/another sweetener
    -Minced ginger
    -Minced garlic
    -Sesame oil
    -Rice vinegar

Salad Ingredients:
Julienned Carrots
Julienned Cucumbers
Red sliced onions - in rings

Directions:
1. Slice the thighs into large chunks and combine with the rest of the fixings in a heat-safe dish. Place foil over the bowl. Add two cups of water to the cooker. Place the steamer rack and bowl on top.
2. Program the Instant Pot for 10 minutes on high pressure with a 10-minute natural release. Then, quick release the pressure.
3. Shred the chicken and enjoy.

White Chicken Chili

Servings: 4
Total Time: 25 min.
Nutrition Facts: 204 Calories| 12 grams Fat| 15 grams Protein|
6 grams Net Carbs

Ingredients:
2 lb. chicken breasts – skinless – boneless
4 diced celery stalks
2 diced onions
10 minced garlic cloves
1-2 minced jalapeno peppers
1 t. of each:
   -Coriander powder
   -Cumin
   -Oregano
1 tbsp. salt – to taste
¼ t. freshly cracked black pepper
1 tbsp. chili powder
4 c. chicken broth
1 pkg. frozen (1 lb.) corn
1 can (15 oz.) cannellini beans – rinsed

For Serving:
Cilantro
Hot Sauce

Directions:
1. Mix everything into the Instant Pot (omit the beans and corn).
2. Secure the lid, and set on high pressure for 15 minutes.
3. Quick release the pressure and shred the chicken in the pot, adding the corn and cannellini beans. Saute for 5 minutes until heated. Serve.

Whole Chicken & Gravy

Yields: 12 Servings: 12
Total Time: 45 min.
Nutrition Facts: 450 Calories| 34.5 grams Protein| 30.2 grams
Fat| 0.7 grams Net Carbs

Ingredients:
6 ½ lb. whole chicken
2 tbsp. olive oil
½ t. of each:
    -Salt
    -Garlic powder
    -Black pepper
    -Onion powder
1 t. dried Italian seasonings
1 ½ c. chicken broth (low-sodium)
2 t. guar gum

Directions:
1. Rub one tbsp. of the oil over the entire chicken, and the rest of the oil into the Instant Pot. Combine the dry seasonings and sprinkle over the entire chicken.
2. Use the saute function to warm the oil, adding the chicken – breast side down. Let it sauté for five minutes, flip, and empty in the chicken broth.
3. Secure the top, and set the timer for 40 minutes (manually). When done, quick release the pressure.
4. Add the chicken to a bowl and prepare the gravy with the guar gum in the hot broth. Stir until thickened. You can add another teaspoon if it isn't thick as you like it.
5. Serve with gravy and a sprinkle of chopped parsley.

Chapter 6: Delicious Dinner Time Meals

You will discover a variety of tasty dishes in this segment!

Cabbage & Corned Beef

Servings: 12
Total Time: 95 minutes
Nutrition Facts: 334 Calories| 23.7 grams Protein| 22.8 grams
Fat| 5.5 grams Net Carbs

Ingredients:
6 c. water
4 lb. corned beef brisket
4 garlic cloves
2 t. black peppercorns
2 t. dried mustard
1 c. sliced - 2 onions
1 c. chopped – 4 celery stalks
1 c. sliced – 4 carrots

Directions:

1. Discard the seasoning packet in the meat package. Arrange the brisket in the Instant Pot. Pour in the water (to cover the brisket), and add the spices.
2. Secure the lid and choose the meat/stew setting (high-60 min.).
3. Natural release the pressure (20 min.) and remove the brisket. Place in foil to keep it warm.
4. Stir in the veggies to the pot and choose the soup function (15 min.). Quick release and add the brisket to the pot. Enjoy!

Carne Adovada

Servings: 10
Total Time: 1 hr. 25 min.
Nutrition Facts: 217 Calories | 21.3 grams Protein |12.3 grams
    Fat | 4.1 grams Net Carbs

Ingredients:
4 lb. pork shoulder – 1-inch pieces
1 tbsp. canola oil
2 c. - chicken broth - low-sodium
8 dried chilis – stemmed & in small bits
1 c. diced onions
2 tbsp. all-purpose flour
6 garlic cloves
Optional:
    -2 chipotle peppers in adobo sauce
    -1 t. kosher salt
1 tbsp. cider vinegar
¼ t. ground cumin
½ t. dried oregano

Directions:
1. Toss the chilies in a heat-proof container. Warm up the broth in a small pan, and pour over the chilis. Let it rest for about 30 minutes.
2. Warm up the pot using the saute function. Cover the pork with flour and saute (in batches) for about 15 minutes.
3. Add the soaked chilies to your blender along with the garlic, broth, and chipotle peppers. Mix until creamy smooth and combine with the onions, chili sauce, salt, cumin, oregano, and vinegar. Pour over the pork.

4. Secure the lid and set the timer for 20 minutes on the high setting. When done, natural release about five minutes, and quick release the rest of the pressure.
5. Remove the lid and serve.

Chipotle Pork Roast

Servings: 4
Total Time: 1 hr. 2 min.
Nutrition Facts: 460 Calories| 40 grams Protein| 31.0 grams Fat| 4 grams Net Carbs

Ingredients:
7 ¼ oz. diced tomatoes - canned
6 oz. bone broth
2 oz. mild diced canned green chilis
2 lb. pork roast
½ t. of each:
   -Cumin
   -Onion powder
1 t. chipotle powder

Directions:
1. Combine all of the ingredients in your Instant Pot.
2. Close the top of the pot and use the manual setting for 60 minutes.
3. Do a natural release of the pressure.
4. Serve and enjoy.

Country-Style Pork Ribs

Yields: 6 Servings: 6 – 3 Ribs
Total Time: 1 hr. 10 min.
Nutrition: 387 Calories| 27 grams Protein| 29 grams Fat| 2 grams Net Carbs

Ingredients:
1 (5 lb.) country style pork ribs

Ingredients for the Rub:
1 tbsp. erythritol/another sweetener
1 t. of each:
  -Paprika
  -Onion powder
  -Garlic powder
½ t. of each:
  -Black pepper
  -Ground coriander
  -Allspice

Ingredients for the Sauce:
2 tbsp. of each:
  -Erythritol/your favorite sweetener

-Red wine vinegar

½ c. reduced-sugar/homemade

¼ c. liquid smoke

½ c. water

½ t. onion powder

½ tbsp. ground of each:

   -Allspice

   -Mustard

¼ t. xanthan gum - optional

Directions:

1. Rub down the ribs with the combined seasonings and stack in the Instant Pot.
2. Mix the sauce fixings and pour over the ribs.
3. Secure the lid and set for 35 minutes (manually) under high pressure.
4. Natural release the pressure and place the ribs in a container to keep warm.
5. Whisk in the xanthan gum (if using) in the Instant Pot, and cook the juices for ten minutes using the saute function.
6. Serve and enjoy!

Cuban Pork

Servings: 10
Total Time: 80 min. (+) Marinade time
Nutrition Facts: 213 Calories | 26.5 grams Protein |9.5 grams Fat | 2 grams Net Carbs

Ingredients:
1 (3 lbs. lean) boneless pork shoulder blade
6 garlic cloves
Juice of 1 lime
Juice of 1 grapefruit – approx. 2/3 c.
1 tbsp. kosher salt
½ tbsp. of each:
   -Cumin
   -Fresh oregano
1 bay leaf

Ingredients for Serving:
Lime Wedges
Hot sauce
Chopped cilantro
Salsa
Tortillas

Directions:
1. Cut up the pork into four chunks and add to a container.
2. Use a blender to combine the juices, garlic, cumin, oregano, and salt; until smooth. Empty over the pork and marinate overnight in the fridge or one hour on the counter (room temperature).
3. Add the fixings to the Instant Pot along with the bay leaf. Secure the lid and cook 80 min (high-pressure).

4. When done, just natural release the pressure. Remove the pork and shred.

5. Remove the juices from the pot and reserve. Arrange the pork back in the Instant Pot along with one cup of the reserved liquid. Keep warm until dinner.

Leg of Lamb

Servings: 8
Total Time: 40 min.
Nutrition Facts: 432 Calories| 44.7 grams Protein| 25.82 grams Fat| 0.64 grams Net Carbs

Ingredients:
1 boneless (3-4 lb.) leg of lamb
2 c. water
2 tbsp. avocado oil – divided
4 crushed garlic cloves
Pepper & Salt to taste
2 tbsp. freshly chopped rosemary

Directions:
1. Dry the lamb using paper towels. Sprinkle with pepper and salt.
2. Use the sauté button to start the Instant Pot, and add the oil. When hot, place the lamb in the pot and brown.
3. Transfer the lamb to a platter and cover with the rosemary and crushed garlic.
4. Add the rack to the pot and arrange the lamb on it. Pour

in the water and select the meat/stew setting. Cook for 30-35 minutes (30 min. for med. rare). Natural release the pressure.

5. Preheat the oven broiler and place the lamb in a pan about six inches from the heat. Two minutes should do the trick. Let it rest about ten minutes and do more slicing.

Mexican Pork Carnitas

Servings: 11
Total Time: Approx. 1 hr. 15 min.
Nutrition Facts: 160 Calories| 20 grams Protein| 7 grams Fat| 1 gram Net Carbs

Ingredients:
2 ½ lb. shoulder blade roast – trimmed and boneless
2 t. kosher salt
Black pepper – to your liking
1 ½ t. cumin
6 minced garlic cloves
½ t. sazon GOYA
¼ t. dry oregano
¾ c. reduced-sodium chicken broth/homemade
2 bay leaves
2-3 chipotle peppers in adobo sauce – to taste
¼ t. dry adobo seasoning – ex. Goya
½ t. garlic powder

Directions:
1. Prepare the roast with pepper and salt. Sear it for about five minutes in a skillet.
2. Let it cool, and insert the garlic slivers into the roast using a blade (approximately one-inch deep). Season with the garlic powder, sazon GOYA, cumin, oregano, and adobo.
3. Arrange the chicken in the Instant Pot, and add the broth, chipotle peppers, and bay leaves. Stir and secure the lid. Prepare using high pressure for 50 minutes (meat button).
4. Natural release the pressure and shred the pork.

Combine with the juices and discard the bay leaves.

5. Add a bit more cumin and adobo if needed. Stir well and serve.

Mutton Curry

Servings: 4
Total Time: 40 min.
Nutrition Facts: 253 Calorie|24.65 grams Protein|13.5 grams Fat|6.34 grams Net Carbs

Ingredients:
3 tbsp. oil/ghee
1 lb. mutton bone-in (1-2-inch bits)
1 large (11 oz.) finely chopped onion
Optional: 1 green chili
½ tbsp. minced of each:
   -Ginger
   -Garlic
1 tbsp. lemon juice
1 med. chopped tomato
Garnish: Cilantro

Spices:
2 t. coriander
1 t. of each:
   -Cayenne/red chili powder
   -Salt
   -Garam masala
¼ t. turmeric

Whole Spices:
6 of each:
   -Cloves
   -Black peppercorns
½ t. cumin seeds
1 bay leaf

1 (1-inch) cinnamon stick

2 black cardamom

Directions:

1. Use the sauté function in the Instant Pot, and pour in the oil. Fold in the whole spices and saute 30 seconds. Stir in the onions, green chilies, and garlic. Sauté for four minutes.

2. Blend in the spices and chopped tomatoes, and stir for another two minutes.

3. Stir in the mutton and mix well, sautéing for another two minutes.

4. Close the lid and change to the meat function for 20 minutes.

5. Natural release the pressure and add the lemon juice. Garnish with the mutton curry and cilantro. Enjoy!

No-Noodle Lasagna

Servings: 8
Total Time: 35 min.
Nutrition Facts: Calories 365| 25 grams Protein |25 grams Fat |
6 grams Net Carbs

Ingredients:
2 minced garlic cloves
1 lb. ground beef
1 small onion
1 large egg
1 ½ c. ricotta cheese
½ c. parmesan cheese
1 jar (25 oz.) marinara sauce
8 oz. sliced mozzarella
Also Needed: 1 ½ quart soufflé/similar dish to fit in pot

Directions:
1. Prepare the Instant Pot using the sauté setting. Brown the beef, onion, and garlic.
2. Meanwhile, combine the parmesan, ricotta, and egg in a separate bowl.
3. Drain the grease from the meat, and add the mixture to the baking dish. Pour in the marinara sauce. Reserve ½ of the meat sauce.
4. Add the ½ of the mozzarella cheese over the meat sauce, ½ of the ricotta cheese and the rest of the sauce. Layer the part of the ricotta cheese on top with a few pieces of mozzarella for the final layer.
5. You can cover with a loose piece of aluminum foil to prevent a condensation buildup on the cheese.
6. Add one cup of water to the Instant Pot and arrange the baking dish on the trivet/rack in the base. You can use a

sling (about 12 inches of foil folded as a handle) for easier removal. Cover and set the timer for 8-10 minutes using the high-pressure setting.

7. Quick release the steam and sprinkle with the parmesan cheese.

8. Cover until the cheese melts and spoon into bowls.

Pork – Noodles & Veggies

Servings: 6
Total Time: 20 min.
Nutrition: 241 Calories| 15 grams Protein| 18 grams Fat| 3 grams Net Carbs

Ingredients:
1 tbsp. oil
1 lb. ground pork
1 c. chopped bell peppers
2 garlic cloves
½ c. chopped onion
4 c. chopped baby spinach
2 pkg. shirataki noodles
½ c. grated parmesan cheese

Directions:

1. Prepare the Instant Pot on the sauté function, and add the oil when hot.
2. Toss in the pork and sauté until slightly pink. Add the garlic, onions, peppers, and spinach. Scrape the browning bits from the bottom and secure the lid.
3. Use the high-pressure setting for three minutes and quick release the pressure. Empty the sauce over the noodles and garnish with the cheese.

Smothered Pork Chops

Servings: 4
Total Time: 36-40 min.
Nutrition Facts: 481.25 Calories | 39.59 grams Protein |32.61 grams Fat | 4.06 grams Net Carbs

Ingredients:
4 boneless (4-6 oz.) pork loin chops
1 tbsp. paprika
1 t. of each:
  -Salt
  -Black pepper
  -Onion powder
  -Garlic powder
¼ t. cayenne pepper
2 tbsp. coconut oil
1 tbsp. butter
6 oz. sliced baby Bella mushrooms
½ med. sliced onion
¼ - ½ t. xanthan gum
½ c. heavy cream
1 tbsp. parsley – freshly chopped

Directions:
1. Combine the cayenne, black pepper, onion powder, salt, garlic powder, and paprika for the rub.
2. Rinse and pat dry the pork. Sprinkle both sides of the meat with 1 tablespoon of the spice rub.
3. Heat up the oil in the Instant Pot using the saute function. Brown the chops three minutes on each side, and add to a platter.
4. Turn off the pot and toss in the mushrooms and onions. Top with the chops and secure the lid. Prepare using the

manual high setting for 25 minutes. You can natural or quick release the pressure.

5. Remove the lid and add the chops back to the platter.

6. Sauté the mixture and whisk in the butter, heavy cream, and the rest of the spices. Sprinkle with the xanthan gum and whisk. Sauté for another three to five minutes until the sauce begins to thicken. Continue adding the xanthan gum until it reaches the desired thickness. It will also thicken as it cools.

7. Top off the chops with the gravy and give it a sprinkle of parsley before serving.

Spicy Pork – Korean Style

Servings: 4
Total Time: 40 min.
Nutrition: 189 Calories| 15 grams Protein| 9 grams Fat| 9 grams Net Carbs

Ingredients:
1 lb. pork shoulder
1 thinly sliced onion
1 tbsp. of each:
   -Minced garlic
   - Minced ginger
   - Soy sauce
   -Sesame oil
   -Rice wine
2 Splenda packs
1 t. Cayenne
2 tbsp. gochugaru
¼ c. water

Ingredients for Finishing:
¼ c. sliced green onion
1 tbsp. sesame seeds
1 thinly sliced onion

Directions:
1. Cut the pork into ¼ - ½- inch slices, and add the rest of the marinade ingredients into a container. Let this rest for 1 hour to 24 hours. When ready to cook, use the high-pressure setting for 20 minutes. Natural release.
2. Use a cast iron skillet to cook the thinly sliced onion and pork cubes. Once the pan is hot, just empty in the sauce, and mix with the pork.
3. When the sauce has cooled down, the onions will be soft. Toss the green onions and sesame seeds and serve.

Vegetarian Butter Chicken with Soy Curls

Servings: 6
Total Time: 20 min.
Nutrition Facts: 254 Calories| 5 grams Protein| 24 grams Fat| 4 grams Net Carbs

Ingredients:
1 c. water
1 ½ cups dry soy curls
1 can (14.5 oz.) diced tomatoes
5-6 garlic cloves
½ t. cayenne pepper
1 t. of each:
   -Ground cumin
   -Garam masala
   -Paprika
   -Salt
   -Turmeric
   -Cayenne pepper
1-2 t. minced ginger

Directions:
1. Add the fixings (water, spices, soy curls, and tomatoes), and cook for 6 minutes under high pressure. Natural release for ten minutes, and follow with a quick release.
2. Switch to the sauté function in the Instant Pot and add the butter.
3. Garnish as you like, and enjoy!

Soups

Cauliflower Bacon & Cheese Soup

Servings: 6
Total Time: 58 min.
Nutrition: 347 Calories| 25.6 grams Fat| 17.7 grams Protein|
13.4 grams Net Carbs

Ingredients:
2 minced garlic cloves
1 large diced onion
1 tbsp. olive oil
1 head coarsely chopped cauliflower
1 tbsp. onion powder
1 chopped green pepper- optional
To Taste: Ground black pepper and salt
32 oz. chicken stock
1 tbsp. Dijon mustard
1 c. Half and Half
6 slices- diced- turkey bacon cooked
2 c. shredded cheddar cheese
Hot pepper sauce- 4 dashes

Directions:

1. Choose the sauté function in the Instant Pot. Add the garlic, onion, and olive oil. Sauté about 3 minutes. When brown, add the green pepper, cauliflower, salt, pepper, and onion powder.
2. Empty the stock, close the lid, and set the timer for 15 minutes.
3. When the timer buzzes, quick release the pressure.
4. Add the Half-and-Half, cheddar cheese, turkey bacon, hot sauce, and Dijon mustard. Cook until bubbly, about 5 minutes. Enjoy.

Ham & Bean Soup

Servings: 6

Total Time: 1 hr. 10 min.

Nutrition: 269 Calories| 21 grams Protein| 14 grams Fat| 13 grams Net Carbs

Ingredients:

1 c. of each:

   -Chopped onion

   -Dried black soybeans – after soaking yields = 2 c. beans

   -Chopped celery

1 t. of each:

   -Dried oregano

   -Cajun seasoning

   -Salt – maybe ½ t.

   -Liquid smoke

   -Louisiana Hot Sauce

4 minced garlic cloves

2 t. all-purpose seasoning

2 smoked ham hocks

2 c. of each:

   -Water

   -Chopped ham

Directions:

1. Add all of the fixings to your Instant Pot and choose the bean/chili function (30 min. high-pressure). Natural release for 10 minutes, and quick release the rest of the pressure.
2. Trash the bone and add the meat back in the soup. Roughly purée some of the soup with an immersion blender.
3. Enjoy piping hot with some hot sauce on the side.

Italian Sausage Kale Soup

Servings: 6
Total Time: 22 min.
Nutrition Facts: 400 Calories| 16 g Protein| 33 g Fat| 8 g Net Carbs

Ingredients:
6 minced garlic cloves
1 c. diced onion
1 lb. hot Italian sausage
12 oz. frozen of each:
   -Kale
   -Cauliflower

Ingredients for Finishing:
½ c. of each:
   -Shredded parmesan cheese
   -Heavy whipping cream

Directions:
1. Remove the sausage from the casing. Prepare the Instant Pot with the sauté function. Add the sausage when it's hot, breaking it apart.
2. Add the garlic, onions, frozen kale, and frozen cauliflower. Add 3 cups of water, and secure the lid.
3. Cook on high pressure 3 minutes, natural release 5 minutes, then quick release.
4. Add the whipping cream and mix until it is the texture you desire. Empty into serving dishes and garnish with some parmesan cheese.

Chapter 7: Side Dishes and Veggies

Add some of these along with your main dishes.

Cauliflower & Cheese

Servings: 4
Total Time: 20 min.
Nutrition Facts: 270 Calories| 11 grams Protein, 21 grams Fat, |
7 grams Net Carbs

Ingredients:
2 tbsp. cream cheese
2 c. riced cauliflower
Salt & Pepper – to taste
½ c. of each:
   -Half & Half
   -Shredded sharp cheddar cheese
1 ½ c. water

Directions:

1. Combine all of the fixings in a heatproof bowl. Cover with foil.
2. Pour the water into the Instant Pot. Add the bowl on the trivet in the pot.
3. Set the timer for five minutes under high pressure. Natural release for ten minutes, then quick release.
4. Warm up the oven broiler, and add the cauliflower on the rack to brown the cheese. Serve when bubbly.

Mashed Potatoes

Servings: 6
Total Time: 30 min.
Nutrition Facts: 98 Calories|0 gram Protein |9.50 grams Fat| 1 grams Net Carbs

Ingredients:
1 ½ c. water
5-6 baking potatoes
½ t. salt
5 garlic cloves
1 tbsp. vegan butter/extra-virgin olive oil
Dash black pepper
Pinch of nutmeg
Dash of thyme/parsley
1 c. full-fat coconut milk
For the Garnish: Fresh chives

Directions:
1. Add the garlic cloves ¼ t. of salt, water, and the cubed potatoes into the Instant Pot. Set four minutes on high pressure. Natural release the pressure, drain well, mashing slightly to help cool.
2. Mince the garlic and add it with the rest of the fixings, salt, and ½ cup of the coconut milk (more if needed). Whip lightly for texture and let it rest.
3. Taste and adjust salt as needed. Top it off with some chives.

Spaghetti Squash

Servings: 4
Total Time: 11 min.
Nutrition Facts: 31 Calories | 0.6 grams Protein | 0.6 grams Fat | 5.5 grams Net Carbs

Ingredients:
1 med. spaghetti squash
1 c. water

Directions:
1. Prepare the spaghetti squash. Cut the squash in half, and scoop out the seeds.
2. Add one cup of water to the Instant Pot.
3. Add the squash (on top of each other) in the pot with the cut-side facing upwards.
4. Secure the lid and prepare for 5 minutes on high pressure. Natural release for five minutes, and quick release the rest of the pressure.
5. Remove the lid carefully and use as desired.

Chapter 8: Brunch & Desserts

Brunch

Deviled Egg Salad

Servings: 5
Total Time: 30 min.
Nutrition Facts: 313.44 Calories | 16.4 grams Protein |26.36 grams Fat | 1.31 grams Net Carbs

Ingredients:
5 raw bacon strips
10 large eggs
2 tbsp. mayo
1 t. Dijon mustard
1 stalk green onion
¼ t. smoked paprika
Pepper & Salt to taste
Also Needed: 6-7-inch cake pan

Directions:
1. Grease all sides of the pan that will sit inside of the pot on the trivet. Pour one cup of cold water in the bottom of the Instant Pot and add the steam rack.
2. Crack the eggs open in the pan (try not to break the yolks).
3. Place the pan on the rack. Secure the lid and set the timer for six minutes (high pressure). Natural release, and remove the pan.

4. Dab away any moisture. Flip the pan on a cutting board for the egg loaf to release. Chop and add to a mixing dish.

5. Clean the Instant Pot bowl and choose the saute function (med. heat). Prepare the bacon until crispy.

6. Add to the chopped eggs with the mustard, mayo, paprika, pepper, and salt. Toss and garnish with green onion.

7. Serve the way you like it!

Egg Cups on the Run

Servings: 4
Total Time: 15 min.
Nutrition Facts: 115 Calories | 9 grams Protein |9 grams Fat | 2 grams Net Carbs

Ingredients:
4 eggs
½ c. sharp shredded cheddar cheese
1 c. diced veggies – ex. tomatoes, mushrooms, etc.
¼ c. Half & Half
Pepper & Salt to taste
2 tbsp. cilantro – chopped

Ingredients for the topping: ½ c. shredded cheese your choice

Also Needed: 4 wide-mouthed jars

Directions:
1. Whisk the veggies, eggs, Half & Half, salt, pepper, cheese, and cilantro.
2. Combine the mixture into each of the jars. Secure the lids (not too tight) to keep water from getting into the egg mix.
3. Pour 2 cups of water into the Instant Pot along with the trivet.
4. Arrange the jars on the trivet and set the timer for 5 minutes (high-pressure). When done, quick release the pressure and top with the rest of the cheese (½ c.).
5. Broil for 2-3 minutes or until the cheese is browned to your liking.

Perfection: The Boiled Egg

Servings: 4
Total Time: 15 min.
Nutrition Facts: 78 Calories |6 grams Protein |5 grams Fat | 0.5 grams Net Carbs

Ingredients:
1 c. water
4 large eggs
Instant Pot trivet

Directions:
1. Pour the water into the pot and add the trivet. Arrange the eggs on the rack, and use the following times:
    a. Soft-Boiled: 3 min. high-pressure
    b. Hard-Boiled: 5 min. high-pressure
2. Quick release the steam and place the eggs in a colander under cold running water. Peel immediately.
3. Use and enjoy!

Desserts
Almond & Coconut Cake

Servings: 8

Total Time: 50 min.
Nutrition Facts: 236 Calories| 5 grams Protein| 23 grams Fat| 3 grams Net Carbs

Dry Ingredients:
1 c. almond flour
½ c. unsweetened shredded coconut
1/3 c. Truvia
1 t. of each:
   -Apple pie spice
   -Baking powder

Wet Ingredients:
¼ c. melted butter
2 lightly whisked eggs
½ c. heavy whipping cream

Also Needed:
1 (6-inch) round cake pan
2 c. water

Directions:
1. Combine all of the 'dry' fixings. Add each of the 'wet' ingredients – one at a time. Empty the batter into the pan, and cover with foil.
2. Empty the water into the Instant Pot, and place the steamer rack.
3. Set the timer 40 minutes using the high-pressure

setting. Natural release for ten minutes. Then, quick release.

4. Remove the pan and let it cool 15 to 20 minutes. Flip it over onto a platter and garnish as desired (count the carbs).

Carrot & Almond Cake

Servings: 8
Total Time: 60 minutes
Nutrition Facts: 268 Calories|25 grams Fat | 6 grams Protein |
4 grams Net Carbs

Ingredients:
3 eggs
2/3 c. swerve
1 c. almond flour
1 ½ t. apple pie spice
1 t. baking powder
¼ c. coconut oil
1 c. shredded carrots
½ c. each of:
   -Heavy whipping cream
   -Chopped walnuts
Also Needed: 6-inch cake pan & hand mixer

Directions:
1. Grease the cake pan. Combine all of the fixings with the mixer until well blended. Pour into the pan and cover with foil.
2. Pour two cups of water into the Instant Pot along with the steamer rack.
3. Arrange the pan on the trivet and set the pot using the cake button (40 min.).
4. Natural release the pressure for ten minutes, and quick release the rest.
5. Place on a rack to cool before frosting. You can also eat plain.

Chocolate Mini Cakes for 2

Servings: 2
Total Time: 15 min.
Nutrition Facts: 193 Calories |15 grams Protein |12 grams Fat |
9 grams Net Carbs

Ingredients:
2 large eggs
2 tbsp. each of:
   -Splenda/your favorite sweetener
   -Heavy cream
½ t. baking powder
¼ c. baking cocoa
1 t. vanilla extract

Directions:
1. Add one cup of water and the trivet to the Instant Pot.
2. Combine all of the dry ingredients and mix well.
3. Mix in another dish, and blend in the rest of the ingredients (eggs, cream, vanilla extract).
4. Spray the ramekins and fill each one halfway. Carefully add them to the cooker and secure the lid.
5. Prepare for nine minutes using the high-pressure setting.
6. Quick release the pressure and add to a plate to cool.

Coconut Pandan Custard – Thai Style

Servings: 4
Total Time: 55 min.
Nutrition Facts: 174 Calories| 6 grams Protein| 14 grams Fat| 6 grams Net Carbs

Ingredients:
3 eggs
1 c. coconut milk - unsweetened
1/3 c. Truvia baking blend/favorite sweetener
3-4 drops vanilla extract/Pandan Extract
2 c. water

Directions:
1. Combine the sweetener, eggs, and Pandan Extract. Empty into a heat-proof (6-inch) bowl. Place foil over the top.
2. Pour the water into the Instant Pot, and add the trivet. Put the bowl in the center of the pot. Set the timer for 30 minutes using high pressure. Natural release the pressure.
3. The custard is set when a knife comes from the center cleanly. Cool in the fridge until chilled and completely set.

Lemon Ricotta Cheesecake

Servings: 6
Total Time: 50 min.
Nutrition Facts: 181 Calories| 5 grams Protein| 16 grams Fat| 2 grams Net Carbs

Ingredients:
8 oz. cream cheese
¼ c. Truvia
1 lemon – Zest and juice
1/3 c. Ricotta cheese
½ t. lemon extract
2 eggs

Ingredients for the Topping:
1 t. Truvia
2 tbsp. sour cream

Also Needed:
A 6-inch springform pan

Directions:

1. Combine all of the fixings in a stand mixer (omit the eggs).
2. Taste test and add the eggs. Use the low speed, since over-beating the eggs will cause the crust to crack.
3. Add the batter to the pan. Cover with foil/silicone lid.
4. Add the trivet and two cups of water and arrange the pan in the Instant Pot.
5. Cook 30 minutes (high-pressure). Natural release the pressure.
6. Blend in the Truvia and sour cream. Decorate the warm cake and place in the fridge to chill for six to eight hours.

Peach & Peanut Butter Chocolate Cheesecake

Servings: 8
Total Time: 23 min.
Nutrition Facts: 191 Calories | 16 grams Fat |4 grams Net Carbs|6 grams Protein

Ingredients:
2 eggs
16 oz. cream cheese
2 tbsp. powdered peanut butter
½ c. swerve sweetener
1 tbsp. cocoa
1 t. vanilla extract

Directions:
1. Note: Prepare the food only when they are at room temperature.
2. Combine the eggs and cream cheese in the blender. Next, add the remainder of the fixings and blend well.
3. Add the mixture to 4 (8 oz.) mason jars. Secure with a lid or foil.
4. Arrange the trivet and add one cup of water to the Instant Pot.
5. Place the jars on the rack and cook in two batches if needed.
6. Prepare using the high-pressure setting for 15-18 minutes.
7. Natural release the pressure and chill overnight or at least several hours.
8. Garnish with a drizzle of peanut butter or a bit of whipped heavy cream. Add a few small bits of chopped peanuts; just count the carbs.

Conclusion

Thanks again for taking the time to download the *Ketogenic Instant Pot Cookbook*! You will discover all of the reasons why this is a great diet, and you will enjoy this enlightening book when you know how it can help with all of these items:

- *Convenience*
- *Energy Efficiency*
- *Dependable & Safe*

The meals are limitless, and you will soon discover what you have been missing out of life with so much less time consumed in food prep. You know this will be a great addition to your cookbook resources. It will surely be frequently used as you plan your weekly meal plans.

You will discover how easy it can be to measure the ingredients and follow the step-by-step information provided for each of the tasty recipes. All you need to do is gather a shopping list of what you need to become ketogenic and head to the superstore for supplies.

Enjoy!

Index for Recipes

Chapter 4: Beef Inspired Meals

Chapter 5: Chicken Inspired Meals

Chapter 6: Delicious Dinner Time Meals

Cabbage & Corned Beef
Carne Adovada
Chipotle Pork Roast
Country-Style Pork Ribs
Cuban Pork
Leg of Lamb
Mexican Pork Carnitas
Mutton Curry
No-Noodle Lasagna
Pork – Noodles & Veggies
Smothered Pork Chops
Spicy Pork – Korean Style
Vegetarian Butter Chicken with Soy Curls

Soups

Cauliflower Bacon & Cheese Soup*
Ham & Bean Soup*
Italian Sausage Kale Soup*

Chapter 7: Side Dishes and Veggies

Cauliflower & Cheese
Mashed Potatoes
Spaghetti Squash

Chapter 8: Brunch & Desserts

Brunch

Deviled Egg Salad
Egg Cups on the Run
Perfection: The Boiled Egg

Desserts

Almond & Coconut Cake
Carrot & Almond Cake
Chocolate Mini Cakes for 2
Coconut Pandan Custard – Thai Style
Lemon Ricotta Cheesecake
Peanut Butter Chocolate Cheesecake